D0461777

NFL DADS

DEDICATED TO

DAUGHTERS

» Inspiring Personal Accounts of Fatherhood «
from the Men of the NFL

EDITED BY LESLIE SATCHELL

TABLE OF CONTENTS

FRIEND | CONFIDANT

CHAMPION | FAN

*The teams listed throughout the book are those the player or coach was with at time of publication.

ACKNOWLEDGMENTS

Tony Porter of **A CALL TO MEN** was the visionary for *NFL Dads Dedicated to Daughters*. We are grateful for his involvement and passion in the area of domestic violence education and prevention as it relates to the men of the NFL. The **NFL Player Development Department** was extremely supportive in getting this project off the ground and investing in the process to deliver a topnotch product. We acknowledge their continued willingness to partner with **Stacy Robinson** and **NFLPA Player Development** to encourage personal development for our players off the field. **Dr. Sara Hickmann** (NY Jets) was the first to realize the vision of Tony Porter and was instrumental in helping to develop the idea for the book. Thank you so much. **Tanya Lumbi** and **Kecia Butlin** of **Forty Forty Agency** were both tremendously perceptive in developing the ideal concept for telling the story of the NFL men and their daughters. We truly appreciate their patience and commitment to making this a very special project. Supreme credit goes to the staff members of the **NFLPA**. This could not have happened without them. **Leslie M. Satchell** (NFLPA Player Development) was the lead on the project and worked tirelessly to coordinate all the moving parts. She remained optimistic and steadfast to see this project through to the very end. Kudos! Thanks to **Joanna Comfort** (formerly of NFLPA Communications), who stuck to the schedule and never complained about going over copy time and time again until it was perfect. From overseeing interview transcription to editing text, she was amazingly proficient. We appreciate the efforts of **Carl Francis** (NFLPA Communications) for supporting promotional events and spreading the word about this unique project to make it a success. Much gratitude goes to **Veronica Jenkins** (NFLPA Communications) for making time to help us sort through a myriad of photographs. Your support was undeniably priceless! To **Steve Goodman**, for lending a hand to execute the business side of the project, we are exceedingly thankful. Without your guidance, the book would never have made it to shelves. Also, thanks to **NFL PLAYERS Player Marketing**, **Kimberly Murray** (NFLPA Player Development), former **NFLPA** interns **Joey Pahira** and **Glendalyn Junio**, team Player Development Directors, professional photographers, personal assistants, agents, wives and families of the participants, and the countless others who helped to take care of the many details. You are the best!

The team at **Triumph Books** was an amazing partner in helping us accomplish our goals. They supported us without fail, helped maintain focus and worked diligently to make this book everything it needed to be. Working with them was indeed a pleasure and we are indebted for such a magnificent experience.

Lastly and most importantly, the NFL Players Association would like to thank **the men of the National Football League** who took their time to be a part of this extraordinary project. We recognize and respect your position as first-rate men, respected figures of the NFL, active fathers, and courageous advocates for ending violence against women. Your willingness to participate is beyond commendable.

DeMaurice Smith, Executive Director, NFLPA

A CALL TO MEN FOREWORD

Engaging men in the fight to end violence against women will impact the world in which we live. Sexism or any other type of ingrained ideology that indicates how men should relate to and treat women indirectly gives abusers license to behave inappropriately. In my work with A CALL TO MEN, I have challenged men all over this country to take a long, hard look in the mirror and address potentially contributory behavior. This, in turn, has caused many of them to reevaluate how they view women. I've met with countless men—from those who serve in the military or pledge fraternities on college campuses to members of community organizations and special interest groups—but no other encounter has been more memorable and gratifying than my time with the men of the National Football League.

Over the last two years, I have had the privilege of working with more than 20 teams as part of the life skills session offered by club Player Development departments, and the response from the players has been not only positive but also quite refreshing. To experience the candor and emotion elicited by a topic often considered to be a "woman's issue" from the most adored and seemingly aggressive athletes in the world was very powerful. But it was the men who had daughters who impressed me the most, in part because of their sincere desire and commitment to being role models, to holding each other accountable, and to inspiring men in their communities to be better fathers, husbands, partners and friends.

Inspired by the players' daughters, the concept for *NFL Dads Dedicated to Daughters* was born. The courageous men of the NFL volunteered to share their thoughts and opinions on what it means to be a real man in today's society while engaging in thoughtful discussions on the role men play in preventing domestic violence. These feelings are interwoven throughout this book with personal accounts of fatherhood and moving photographs of their daughters. Much like the players, the NFL Players Association and the National Football League hope that those who read the genuine expressions of these influential men will be encouraged to find their own voice and to stand up and speak out on this important issue with the same fervor and passion. Historically, women have been at the forefront of addressing matters of domestic violence, but it is my belief (and the belief of A CALL TO MEN) that well-meaning men—those who avoid abusive relationships—have a role in prevention. I commend the men of the NFL for taking on this responsibility and tackling the issue of violence against women.

Tony Porter, Co-Founder A CALL TO MEN

INTRODUCTION

Football naturally makes you think about fans, field goals, friends, and even the five-yard line. Now, the National Football League Players Association and the National Football League want you to associate football with fathers as well. Our beloved game entertains millions of people each year, as it remains the number one sport in the U.S. But it's important to understand that the lives of its players are about so much more than just playing the game. Fatherhood and family drive and inspire NFL players to compete and press toward accomplishing their goals on and off the field. It is particularly heartwarming to experience the emotion in a room full of strapping, hard-hitting football players and to feel the passion that pours from their souls when they speak about their daughters. This view of the men we love to watch make big plays, rejoice with showy touchdown celebrations, and vie for a chance to play in the Super Bowl is one fans rarely get to see. But the NFLPA and the NFL want to share a different side of our players. With this book, we want to give you a peek into the lives and the character of the men who make the game of football great.

Though he may wear a helmet on Sunday, the average player's headgear is much different the other six days of the week. Switching effortlessly from wearing an athlete's hat to a father's hat is an art that our players take seriously. Players earn many accolades for their exploits on the field, but being a Teacher/Student, Provider/Protector, Friend/Confidant, and Champion/Fan for their child is the role for which the players in this book most want to be remembered. Super Bowl rings and championship trophies cannot replace the sparkle in the eye of a daughter who looks with love to the man she only knows as "Dad." These players know what really matters, and being a great father is the legacy they want to leave behind for their families. They also understand the influence they have on other men and want to impress upon others the importance of being an active and consistent presence in the lives of children.

Our NFL Dads love all of their children, but this book is truly Dedicated to Daughters. In the spirit of this special, treasured father-daughter relationship and in an attempt to affect the world in which they live, this book showcases some of the most devoted fathers in our league. Their candor is refreshing, their devotion to family is steadfast, and their love for their daughters knows no boundaries.

Leslie Satchell, Manager, Player Development, NFLPA

INSPIRE

Motivate

EDUCATE

GUIDE

ENLIGHTEN

PREPARE

NURTURE

TEACHER | STUDENT

I want my daughters to be independent and strong so they don't ever have to depend on anyone to make them happy.

- TORRY HOLT

My hope for our young men is that they learn
how to handle their emotions appropriately
and respect every woman in their life.

I LOVE HAVING A DAUGHTER,

AND I TAKE PLEASURE IN WATCHING HER GROW.

JEROME BETTIS

RAMS, STEELERS : FORMER PLAYER

I know that my role is to provide certain things for my daughter, but it's so amazing to experience what she does for me as a man. Having her in my life has helped to shape me into who I am today. I am a lot more giving, compassionate, and patient because her very nature has pushed me to become more in tune with my softer side. I don't even have to see her; I can just think about her and my heart just melts. Each time I try fall back into the routine of what society defines as "manly" behavior, the look on my daughter's face, her smile, and sometimes her laugh reminds me that it's okay to be sensitive and vulnerable. I love having a daughter, and I take pleasure in watching her grow. Each and every experience we share strengthens our relationship, and I am grateful that she looks to me for security and confirmation as her father.

I look forward to the day where all men take fatherhood seriously. Our daughters and sons needs to witness appropriate male/female interaction regularly. Advising, talking, and lecturing needs to be accompanied by consistent examples in their lives. I teach my daughter the value of respect and honor by how her treat her every day. I pray that she, and other young women, learn to understand that solid moral character and consistency makes a man—not material items or words without action. Similarly, my hope for our young men is that they learn how to handle their emotions appropriately and respect every woman in their life. Our kids should be learning these lessons from their own fathers first, but also from other men in the community. As men, we need to raise the bar.

ANDRA DAVIS

DENVER BRONCOS : MIDDLE LINEBACKER

Violence against women is a very serious crime. I felt that I had to be a part of this book because getting players involved can really have an effect and help people. Kids idolize us. So we can show them that it's cool to respect women, other people, and themselves.

Sometimes I hear guys use degrading words when they talk about women. It's unnecessary, and I make a point to challenge them on their language. Taking a stand on how men treat women is important to me, because I have three daughters who mean more to me than words can express. For their sake and the sake of the other special women in my life, I'd like to see more God-fearing men who are outwardly convicted to do the right thing no matter what other people think.

I use my grandparents as an example for my life. The way my grandfather treats my grandmother influences how I treat my wife. I want to set the same example for my daughters, so they can experience, firsthand, how a woman should be honored, valued, and appreciated.

Taking a stand on how men treat women is important to me, because I have three daughters who mean more to me than words can express.

I WANT TO SET THE SAME EXAMPLE FOR MY DAUGHTERS,
SO THEY CAN EXPERIENCE FIRSTHAND HOW A WOMAN
SHOULD BE HONORED, VALUED, AND APPRECIATED.

HONESTY, FAIRNESS, AND RESPECT ARE THE QUALITIES
I WANT MY DAUGHTERS TO OBSERVE IN ME.

I actually wear the number 17 because it is the date
of my first daughter's birthday, and she was
born after 17 hours of labor.

JAKE DELHOMME

CLEVELAND BROWNS : QUARTERBACK

Being a dad is extremely special, and I can admit that my daughters have me wrapped around their little fingers. I actually wear the number 17 because it is the date of my first daughter's birthday, and she was born after 17 hours of labor. So even when football takes me away from my girls, I am constantly reminded of the unique place they have in my heart and in my life.

My daughters have helped me grow into a selfless man, who knows that putting your family first is a huge undertaking, but it is the right thing to do as a good man and a good father. I want to be the best father I can be because my girls deserve nothing less. I am incredibly grateful that my dad taught me how demonstrating appropriate behavior is just as important as talking about what's right and wrong. Honesty, fairness, and respect are the qualities I want my daughters to observe in me. Likewise, I would like to see other men demonstrate those characteristics as well. It's the only way to impact our society and potentially end unnecessary mistreatment of all people, especially women.

Instead of being physically tough alone, I wish men would also be mentally strong enough to control their emotions. The patience a man shows with his own daughters, mothers, and sisters is the same patience he should exhibit toward every other woman he encounters.

TONY GONZALEZ

ATLANTA FALCONS : TIGHT END

Like it or not, we're looked at as role models, and it is important that we lead by example. It starts at home, so I am setting the foundation for my kids. But I also want to have a positive influence on the younger generation because their bad decisions could affect us all. I want a better world for my daughter, and if I can have a positive effect on the world, I believe that's a very powerful gift.

Reality TV, media, and music cannot set the standard. It's going to take men, women, parents, and others who are around young kids to show them the proper way to treat women. Honoring commitment and demonstrating healthy love and affection between a man and a woman will be more powerful than just lecturing young people. Actions speak louder than words.

Honoring commitment and demonstrating healthy love and affection between a man and a woman will be more powerful than just lecturing young people.

I REALIZE HOW IMPORTANT IT IS FOR ME TO BE IN TOUCH WITH MY OWN EMOTIONS, SO THAT I CONVEY ALL SIDES OF A GOOD MAN.

Their love, care, concern, and affection make me feel like a king,

and I do all that I can do to live up their expectations.

BRIAN MITCHELL

REDSKINS, EAGLES, GIANTS : FORMER PLAYER

Raising girls is a unique experience that brings me a lot of joy by reminding me every day how blessed I am. I treat each of them like a princess because I want them to understand how special they are, and I am touched by how they take care of me in return. Their love, care, concern, and affection make me feel like a king, and I do all that I can do to live up their expectations.

The values I want my daughters to understand about men and love push me to be the living example for them. I talk about love, respect, integrity, and consistency, but I also show them how these things manifest in the relationship I have with my wife. As a father, I have to process stress, anger, fear, and disappointment appropriately so that I can share these experiences with my daughters. I realize how important it is for me to be in touch with my own emotions, so that I convey all sides of a good man.

After I'm done raising my daughters, they will be on their own in the world. I want them to be safe and secure without having to worry about aggressive or controlling men. It's not always easy for men to confront each other on issues that are considered personal. But we need to step outside of our comfort zone to address domestic violence in our locker rooms, barbershops, schools, and even with within our families in order for things to change.

ANTHONY EDWARDS

ARIZONA CARDINALS : PLAYER DEVELOPMENT DIRECTOR

Before a man can treat a woman with the respect she deserves, he has to first love himself. When a man doesn't love himself, he cannot truly love anyone else.

A real man is one of integrity, purpose, and hard work and one who knows his own God-given identity. A man who serves others is honorable and selfless, and the world needs more men like this. As the saying goes, people would rather see a servant than hear a servant any day.

Men need to walk the walk and talk the talk to gain credibility and keep the attention of young people. That is the best way to teach and change behavior. We should not sit back and judge or criticize; we need to build men up and not tear them down.

A REAL MAN IS A ONE OF INTEGRITY, PURPOSE, AND HARD WORK AND ONE WHO KNOWS HIS OWN GOD-GIVEN IDENTITY.

My daughter means the world to me. She is my princess.

I TREAT EVERYONE WITH RESPECT, ESPECIALLY WOMEN.
I DO SO FOR MY DAUGHTERS TO SEE.

BRIAN WATERS

KANSAS CITY CHIEFS : OFFENSIVE GUARD

As men, we live by the code that tells us to stay out of other people's business. But, we can't continue to do that if violence against women is going to stop. We are definitely at a point where it needs to be a national conversation—first in your home, within your circle of friends, with your brothers, and even your teammates. We all know someone who has an issue with mistreating women. Maybe they haven't admitted it to themselves, but maybe they will with the help of good men.

My relationship with my daughters is so special. Their tenderness awakened a different side of me. I treat everyone with respect, especially women. I do so for my daughters to see, but also for the other females I come into contact with who may be looking at me as an example.

My relationship with my daughters is so special. Their tenderness awakened a different side of me.

BRAD MEESTER

JACKSONVILLE JAGUARS : CENTER

My girls are my world. Having daughters has inspired me to be a better father and a better husband. I think kids watch and learn so much from their parents. As a result, I want to be a better person so that they are better people. I try to set that example in the way I treat my wife, so they know what a man should be like and how a guy should treat them.

It is important for men to teach each other what is appropriate and what is not appropriate when it comes to women. I hope that we can continue to influence the younger generation of men to treat women the right way—to always love them and treat them with the utmost respect.

I hope that we can continue to influence the younger generation of men to treat women the right way—to always take them and treat them with the utmost respect.

MY GIRLS ARE MY WORLD.
I WANT TO BE A BETTER PERSON
SO THAT THEY ARE BETTER PEOPLE.

I THOUGHT I RESPECTED WOMEN,
BUT HAVING DAUGHTERS
TOOK IT TO ANOTHER LEVEL.

CHRIS HOVAN

TAMPA BAY BUCCANEERS : DEFENSIVE TACKLE

I thought I respected women, but having daughters took it to another level. My daughters have taught me to embrace my sensitive side, to be a better listener and supporter, and to be patient.

I have pictures of my wife and children all over my locker at work. Every so often, when I walk in the room, I catch the younger, single guys standing there admiring my collages. I always tell them, "This is my strength, what keeps me going each day, practice after practice, game after game, year after year. In one, five, ten years from now, football will be a memory, but family...that's the real deal!"

My daughters have taught me

to embrace my sensitive side,

be a better listener and supporter,

and to be patient.

JAMES BROWN

THE NFL TODAY, INSIDE THE NFL : HOST

My daughter's smile and personality light up a room and definitely light up my heart. She's not only an excellent mother, but she is also very loving and compassionate. I admire her love for people and her desire to help those who are less fortunate or who may be in need. She's actually helped me in many situations. I remember at her wedding reception I was told by so many how angry I looked walking her down the aisle. I wasn't angry at all—I was just trying not to cry. Later during our father-daughter dance, my daughter told me, "Don't cry, Daddy. It's okay." On her day, she was comforting me. I love her for that.

I want my daughter to be able to come to me for any and all things. My role as a father is to be loving and nurturing, but I also strive to be a teacher as well. I engage my daughter in discussions that will hopefully impart many life lessons.

Self control in all situations is appropriate with an attitude of love governing our actions. We should be quick to hear, slow to speak, and even slower to anger.

My daughter's smile and personality light up a room and definitely light up my heart.

SELF CONTROL IN ALL SITUATIONS IS APPROPRIATE
WITH AN ATTITUDE OF LOVE GOVERNING OUR ACTIONS.

I WANT MY DAUGHTERS TO FIND PEACE
AND CONTENTMENT IN THEIR LIVES.

HEATH EVANS

NEW ORLEANS SAINTS : FULLBACK

I want my daughters to find peace and contentment in their lives through their relationship with Jesus Christ. Life is about blessing and encouraging others!

This world tells our young men that they are weak if they show fear and emotions instead of teaching them how to deal with their feelings. All this does is create a bunch of insecure adult males that misuse their aggressive nature to mask their own fears, insecurities and inadequacies.

I hope that every young man who reads this will be encouraged to be a real man, a man who is committed to his wife and his children, no matter what the cost. I hope every young woman who reads this will hold the men in her own life to a standard that is second to none.

This world tells our young men that they are weak if they show fear and emotions instead of teaching them how to deal with their feelings.

CHRIS KELSAY

BUFFALO BILLS : DEFENSIVE END

Men are taught not to get into other people's business, but the statistics prove that we need to. Part of my responsibility as a Christian is to allow my life to be an example for my daughters and others around me, whether that's in the locker room or anywhere else. I hope I inspire other men to be better.

Leaders have to challenge the messages on TV and the music lyrics that use demeaning language to talk about women. Every woman is someone's mother, daughter, sister, wife or girlfriend, and should be treated and talked about with respect.

I try to spend time with my daughters every day to show how much I care about them. I recognize that I will be the first real man in their lives. My role is very important.

I recognize that I will be the first real man in their lives. My role is very important.

EVERY WOMAN IS SOMEONE'S MOTHER, DAUGHTER,
SISTER, WIFE, OR GIRLFRIEND AND SHOULD BE TREATED
AND TALKED ABOUT WITH RESPECT.

My daughters have brought out a softer, more senstive side of me.

TORRY HOLT

JACKSONVILLE JAGUARS : WIDE RECEIVER

My daughters have brought out a softer, more sensitive side of me. I show them love and respect all of the time, and I have definitely become more of a protector.

I want my daughters to be independent and strong, so they don't ever have to depend on anyone to make them happy.

They definitely inspire me to be the best.

Educating young men early could help to curb violence against women. My mom started teaching me the way I was supposed to behave toward women by insisting on specific behavior when interacting with my sisters. Setting the proper foundation at home was the key for me, and I believe it could have a positive effect on young men as well.

EDUCATING YOUNG MEN EARLY
COULD HELP CURB VIOLENCE AGAINST WOMEN.
SETTING THE PROPER FOUNDATION AT HOME IS THE KEY.

IAN SCOTT

SAN DIEGO CHARGERS : DEFENSIVE TACKLE

As a man, you can be tough. But as a father, you must be able to provide a loving environment for your children. I show my kids that I love them in every way possible.

Young men need to know that you cannot just expect mom to do everything for you. When I was young we all had to help out around the house doing the things that some people consider to be a "woman's job." Learning how to respect my mother and her responsibilities has helped me learn how to respect all women.

There are so many bad examples of how men treat women in music and television, which means good men need to work extra hard to challenge those messages. I don't want the media to set the example for my daughters. That's my job.

I show my kids that I love them in every way possible.

AS A FATHER, YOU MUST BE ABLE TO PROVIDE
A LOVING ENVIRONMENT FOR YOUR CHILDREN.

AS A FATHER, I TRY TO DISPLAY A MAN
THAT IS RESPONSIBLE.

La'ROI GLOVER

RAIDERS, SAINTS, COWBOYS, RAMS : FORMER PLAYER

Hopefully my daughters will choose a man that will have some of the same qualities that I have tried to impress upon them. As a father, I try to display a man that is responsible, pays the bills, provides for his family, shows love and support, and can be a disciplinarian without using hurtful language.

As a father you have to remember that girls can be more sensitive than boys. It's just a different dynamic. I have learned this from my relationship with my daughters—I try to be more selective in the words I use and the context in which I use them. My daughters will always know that I love them from the way that I speak to them. My words and affection come from a place of love in my heart.

My daughters will always know that I love them...
My words and affection come from
a place of love in my heart.

MATT STOVER

INDIANAPOLIS COLTS : KICKER

Boys think that athletic ability, finances, or how many women you have defines what being a man is about. But real men accept responsibility, reject passivity, and live courageously. Men watch the behavior of their peers, just like they do in the locker room. So if you're going to talk about respecting women and living the right way, it's important to back that up with how you conduct yourself.

A father fills his daughter's need for that connection she can only get with a male. If he can do that, she won't look for love in all the wrong places. She'll have it filled by you, her father. I strive to make my daughter feel secure with me to prevent her from confusing an abusive situation with love.

The number one thing that I have in my life that helps me be a man is my wife. I've got a woman who will not let me be a jerk. She holds me accountable, and accountability is key to be the man God intended me to be.

If you're going to talk about respecting women and living the right way, it's important to back that up with how you conduct yourself.

I STRIVE TO MAKE MY DAUGHTER FEEL SECURE.

IT'S IMPORTANT THAT YOUNG GIRLS SEE
POSITIVE RELATIONSHIPS BETWEEN MEN AND WOMEN.

KRIS WILSON

SAN DIEGO CHARGERS : TIGHT END/FULLBACK

Stopping domestic violence is an important cause. If enough people take action, it could really change things. Men are taught to handle problems in an aggressive manner, but when it comes to dealing with women, men must learn to exercise restraint. It doesn't matter who started it; it doesn't matter who's provoking it. The bottom line is it's up to you, as a man, to take responsibility for your actions.

My little girl warms my heart, and being her father is a priceless experience. It's important that young girls see positive relationships between men and women in their lives. My role as the father of a daughter is to show her a positive example of what a man is supposed to be: a positive influence.

My little girl warms my heart, and being her father is a priceless experience.

LORENZO ALEXANDER

WASHINGTON REDSKINS : DEFENSIVE TACKLE

A lot of guys have the wrong role models and get caught up in the culture of the street that says disrespecting women and sleeping around is cool. I think this project is a great opportunity to show the NFL, the community, and the fans that there are many black males who are very passionate about being fathers and take pride in doing the right thing.

It's the responsibility of good men, and fathers like myself, to pull away from the negative stereotypes and model how good men should treat women. Getting my relationship right with God and using the Bible as a foundation to guide my choices has helped me live correctly. I take it upon myself to behave in a way I would want another man to treat my daughter: with love and respect. Being a father is a weighty responsibility, but it's one that brings me great joy.

It's the responsibility of good men,
and fathers like myself,
to pull away from the negative stereotypes.

BEING A FATHER IS A WEIGHTY RESPONSIBILITY,
BUT IT'S ONE THAT BRINGS ME GREAT JOY.

MY WIFE OF 25 YEARS IS MY ROLE MODEL,

AND I HOPE MY CHILDREN EVENTUALLY EMULATE

THE RELATIONSHIP WE DISPLAY AT HOME.

COACH RICHARD BISACCIA

TAMPA BAY BUCCANEERS : ASSOCIATE HEAD COACH

Women are diligent, organized, compassionate, and filled with passion and drive—just like men.

Unfortunately, men often view women through the negative lens of the media and fail to treat them with the respect they deserve. Women are positive role models in many areas of our society. My wife of 25 years is my role model, and I hope my children eventually emulate the relationship we display at home.

It can be difficult for kids today with all the new technology available. There is computer dating and social networking sites—stuff I was never exposed to. But even if a parent has never dealt with all of the new media, they have to monitor it and discuss it with their kids. I often talk with my daughters as well as my son about how to build a relationship from the ground up. Communication and being able to articulate are vital in our society and are things I stress with my children.

Communication and being able to articulate are vital in our society and are things I stress with my children.

MATT TURK

HOUSTON TEXANS : PUNTER

Coming from a broken home without a father figure doesn't give you a pass to mistreat people. Have an open mind and be willing to change.

Growing up, I didn't have a good role model to develop the proper attitude toward women. So for me, breaking the chain started when I gave my life to Christ and began to pursue what God's word told me.

I am blessed to have three daughters and it's my responsibility as a father to be the best example I can be. I certainly treat my wife with respect, but I also show that same respect to other women, whether they're a waitress in a restaurant or a secretary in an office. Men should understand that kids learn from our language and attitude toward people so, no matter their gender or race, we must be thoughtful about the values we represent.

I am blessed to have three daughters and it's my responsibility as a father to be the best example I can be.

I WANT HER TO FIND SOMEONE

WHO HAS RESPECT AND DIGNITY FOR WHO SHE IS

AND WHAT SHE BELIEVES IN.

CHAD GREENWAY

MINNESOTA VIKINGS : LINEBACKER

I think as a man, you should always respect women. My wife is an integral part of our family function, and without her we would be lost. The women in our lives should be celebrated for not only the great people they are, but also for the great things they do every day. You are not a man if you cannot respect women for who they are, and you certainly are not a man if you lay your hands on a woman.

Having a daughter reinforces the ideals my parents instilled in me, which are the same ones I want to give my daughter. I want her to be treated the way I treat my wife, mother, and sisters. I want her to find someone who has respect and dignity for who she is and what she believes in. I want to be that example for her every day.

The women in our lives should be celebrated for not only the great people they are, but also for the great things they do every day.

SUPPORT

DEFEND

NOURISH

SUSTAIN

PREPARE

BOLSTER

COMFORT

PROVIDER | PROTECTOR

I want to be their refuge.

— BRIAN DAWKINS

THERE ARE LEGAL CONSEQUENCES FOR VIOLENT ACTIONS,
BUT THERE SHOULD BE SOCIAL
RAMIFICATIONS AMONGST MEN AS WELL.

DONOVAN McNABB

PHILADELPHIA EAGLES : QUARTERBACK

I realize that young people need to hear from us because they respect us for what we do, but there are a lot of adults who need us to be role models for them as well.

We cannot continue to support a man who needs to dominate a woman in order to boost his own confidence and feel like a man. There are legal consequences for violent actions, but there should be social ramifications amongst men as well. Any respect for a man who puts his hands on a woman should be null and void.

I am very protective of my daughters as well as my wife, and it's frightening to hear the statistics of violence against women. We need to bring this topic up more often and talk about it in a light where people can understand it and feel comfortable sharing so that they can get help. I want my family to live happy, healthy lives in a world where there are good men who treat women right.

I am very protective of my daughters.

I want my family to live happy, healthy lives in a world where there are more good men who treat women right.

KEVIN MAWAE

TENNESSEE TITANS : CENTER

The responsibility that comes with parenting can be overwhelming, but it is rewarding to see your children grow and flourish. My accomplishments on the football field are a blessing, but in the end, I want to be remembered for the kind of father, husband, and man that I am. My faith drives how I treat people, especially my wife and children, and I hope that my actions will influence the younger generation. As a veteran player and a leader, I am aware that others may be watching me, so I take the responsibility of being a good example very seriously.

I treasure the special connection that I have with my daughter and I know how important it is for me to nurture our relationship. When I was growing up, my parents were very affectionate and I am thankful for that experience because it has made me comfortable with being expressive and showing emotion within my own household. Too many men feel like they have to be rough and tough all of the time; however, being a healthy father and man is about learning how to achieve balance. Stern or aggressive behavior is easy for us. But being gentle, loving, and compassionate is a sign of maturity.

With a successful marriage approaching 17 years and an expectation of respect within our family, I am living in a way that shows how much I value women in my personal life. Yet, having a daughter has absolutely opened my eyes to issues outside of our home. I decided to participate in this book project because, as a father who loves his daughter, I realize that she will be on her own one day. I want every man to love and cherish her the way I do; to protect, honor, and respect her with same passion that I have since the day she was born. My hope is that more men will stand up and speak out on violence against women for the sake of their daughters as well.

The responsibility that comes with parenting can be overwhelming, but it is rewarding to see your children grow and flourish.

STERN OR AGGRESSIVE BEHAVIOR IS EASY FOR US. BUT BEING GENTLE, LOVING, AND COMPASSIONATE IS A SIGN OF MATURITY.

My daughters move me to be more loving and compassionate.
They continue to bless me.

DAVID TYREE

BALTIMORE RAVENS : WIDE RECEIVER

To me, being a great father to my daughters means using this great opportunity as an athlete to be a positive voice and prayerfully an inspiration to many.

When I think about my daughters growing up, my prayer is that the men of this world will throw the evil form of pride aside that doesn't allow us to really listen to women and make the proper decisions.

The pride of a man should speak to dignity, not self-righteousness. We have to be men of true love and understand the essence of what love is. Love is pure—it's not afraid to cry; it's not afraid to be in touch with emotions; it's not afraid to reach out; it shows compassion; it gives.

My daughters move me to be more loving and compassionate. They continue to bless me.

THE PRIDE OF A MAN SHOULD SPEAK TO DIGNITY, NOT SELF-RIGHTEOUSNESS.

WALT HARRIS

SAN FRANCISCO 49ERS : CORNERBACK

Having three daughters changed my life in a way that I never expected. When they were born, I immediately became cognizant of the problems in society that could affect them at some point, and domestic violence was one of them. The statistics are alarming, and I think that more men should speak out about it in order for things to change, especially men who are in a position to influence others. Silence could be interpreted as acceptance, and I want my daughters to grow up knowing that daddy had an interest in every aspect of their lives and that I am doing everything in my power to protect them.

My daughters are precious and deserve to be treated accordingly. I recognize that they watch and learn from what I do and what I don't do, so my role as their father and the first man in their lives is very powerful. I take this responsibility seriously and appreciate every opportunity I have to impart principles of faith and how they should expect to give and receive love. Saying *I love you* is extremely important, but showing love is essential as well.

When they were born, I immediately became cognizant of the problems in society that could affect them at some point and domestic violence was one of them.

SAYING *I LOVE YOU* IS EXTREMELY IMPORTANT,
BUT SHOWING LOVE IS ESSENTIAL AS WELL

I WANT MY DAUGHTERS TO KNOW
HOW MUCH I LOVE THEM AND CARE ABOUT THEM EVERY DAY.

I hope this book raises awareness
and clears up our position as players on this issue.

SHANE LECHLER

OAKLAND RAIDERS : PUNTER

I want my daughters to know how much I love them and care about them every day. I try to leave bad practices or games at work because when I come home, my focus is my family.

My goal is to be involved when I can in everything they do and to nurture their unique personalities. My oldest is incredibly outspoken and is very helpful with her sister. But my youngest is more quiet and reserved and likes to entertain herself. My relationship with them is very special to me.

Always publicizing negative behavior of NFL players is unfair because the rest of us get labeled, too. So I think it's important to be involved in projects like this to change that perception by showing the good we do and that most of us do the right thing.

Domestic violence is way too common, and I hope that this book raises awareness and clears up our position as players on this issue.

DESHEA TOWNSEND

PITTSBURGH STEELERS : CORNERBACK

The true measure of a man is whether he can back up his words with actions. No one is perfect, but keeping my daughters in mind as I move through this world helps me stay focused and remember my purpose as a father. Being confident, commanding, powerful, and assertive is expected of me as a man. But having daughters led me to grow in other areas. I am now more patient, loving, expressive, and I have matured in my relationship with God because I know that it's important for my daughters to see me "walking the talk."

The statistics of domestic violence in this country are staggering. Awareness should drive us all reflect on how we can make a difference and impact the lives of women now and for years to come. We cannot only be concerned with the people in our families; as good men, we must shape the perspective of the youth as well. If I can convey that treating a woman with respect is just as important to me as winning football games, I will know that I have done my part.

This project is very meaningful to me because I love my daughters so much and want them to have a life that is free of violence and intimidation. For the well-being of all of our daughters, I hope that more men will speak up on this issue and hold their sons, brothers, fathers, cousins, and teammates accountable for their actions. Showing love, dealing with feelings, handling rejection, and tempering aggression are all things that men need to do better.

THE TRUE MEASURE OF A MAN
IS WHETHER HE CAN BACK UP HIS WORDS WITH ACTIONS.

I love my daughters so much
            and want them to have a life
that is free of violence and intimidation.

My daughter has a beautiful spirit,
and our play time brings out the kid in me.

BRANDON MOORE

NEW YORK JETS : OFFENSIVE LINEMAN

My daughter has a beautiful spirit, and our play time brings out the kid in me. The fact that she is so innocent and tickled by the simplest things reminds me to slow down and take time to appreciate the important things in life. Before she was born, I put so much energy into my career. Although that's still important, I realize that my family and their happiness are my first priority.

Being a dad to a daughter really made me think about women differently. Portrayal of women on TV, locker-room talk, and stories of abuse really worry me, because I want to protect my daughter from experiencing these things. I may have been passive in the past, but now I feel compelled to be more vocal about what's unacceptable. More secure and honorable men should be moved to do the same so that our daughters can grow up in a world where men value and respect women without pause. Speaking up and out is an investment in their future.

THE FACT THAT SHE IS SO INNOCENT AND TICKLED BY THE SIMPLEST THINGS REMINDS ME TO SLOW DOWN AND TAKE TIME TO APPRECIATE THE IMPORTANT THINGS IN LIFE.

ARTHUR HIGHTOWER

SAN DIEGO CHARGERS : DIRECTOR OF PLAYER DEVELOPMENT

My roles as a strong father and as an example for the players I work with made me want to be a part of this project. As men, we have to be more responsible and accountable for our behavior—first to our families but also as men in society.

The statistics don't lie. Domestic violence is a huge issue and even though our daughters may be too young to be affected by it now, they will grow up in a world where this issue impacts many, many women.

If you know someone who has aggression issues, pull him aside, tell him it's not acceptable, show him the right way, and strongly suggest he get help. We need to teach other men and young boys that there is an appropriate way to handle emotions. But violence is not the answer. I want to safeguard this world for our daughters.

My daughters know what to expect from any relationship. My love for them has set the bar high.

My daughters know what to

expect from any relationship.

My love for them

has set the bar high.

VIOLENCE IS NOT THE ANSWER.

I WANT TO SAFEGUARD

THIS WORLD FOR OUR DAUGHTERS.

I HOPE THAT SEEING THE PLAYERS ADDRESS

THIS ISSUE WILL MOVE MEN TO CHALLENGE THEMSELVES.

BRIAN DAWKINS

DENVER BRONCOS : SAFETY

My daughters are a blessing and they bring a lot of joy to my life.

I want to be their refuge and protect them from harm.

Every man should think of the women he encounters as his own sister, mother, or daughter to keep his actions in perspective. I hope that seeing NFL players address this issue will move men to challenge themselves and their peers to deal with emotions and aggression in a healthy way.

My daughters are a blessing, and they bring a lot of joy to my life.

I want to be their refuge and protect them from harm.

DeMARCUS WARE

DALLAS COWBOYS : OUTSIDE LINEBACKER

People look at us as players, but don't always see the family men that many of us are. My daughter is my heart, and she inspires me to make sure that I model the values of a good man. I want her to see in me a man of integrity who is loyal and loving, so that she knows what to expect from other men when she gets older. I want to protect her from anything and anybody who may hurt her.

I do understand that the world has changed, but we should be doing things to show the women in our lives how much we love and cherish them, not that we want to control or hurt them.

The statistics on assault blow my mind. We really have to start showing boys what it means to be a real man—how to be self-sufficient, how to get a job, how to love their wives and families, and how to appreciate life.

WE SHOULD BE DOING THINGS TO SHOW THE WOMEN
IN OUR LIVES HOW MUCH WE LOVE AND CHERISH THEM.

My daughter is my heart, and she inspires me.

I want to protect her from anything

and anybody who may hurt her.

I WANT MY DAUGHTER TO GROW UP IN A WORLD WHERE

MEN RESPECT HER AND TAKE HER SERIOUSLY.

I TEACH HER TO EXPECT ONLY THE BEST.

CHESTER PITTS

HOUSTON TEXANS : OFFENSIVE GUARD

People assume that because we're aggressive on the field, we condone aggressiveness in other areas, which is far from the truth. I want my daughter to grow up in a world where men respect her and take her seriously. Any type of abuse, verbal or physical, is not acceptable. I model appropriate behavior toward women, and I teach my little girl to expect only the best.

Men should let go of the macho idea that says you're soft if you don't dominate and control women or if you choose to step in when you see a woman being mistreated. The men who mistreat women are cowards, and it's up to the good men to set the standard.

Men should let go of the macho idea that says you're soft if you don't dominate and control.

COACH JIM MORA Jr.

SEATTLE SEAHAWKS : HEAD COACH

The examples we set in how we treat our wives, our mothers, and our daughters are tremendously important. Young people are paying attention, and more men need to be brave enough to take a stand.

When we hear other men talking about women as objects rather than people, we have to be willing to step out of our comfort zone and speak out against it. Professional sports can sometimes foster a sexist atmosphere, but the only way to move past that is by challenging people.

It's important to bring light to the issue of domestic violence and the experience of women because, as men, we don't always have a great appreciation of what women go through.

Having a young daughter and knowing how men can be made me want to participate in this project. When she goes to high school and then off to college, I want her to feel safe in an environment where men respect her morals and integrity. My daughter embodies great self-respect and my hope is that she will be treated accordingly.

YOUNG PEOPLE ARE PAYING ATTENTION, AND
MORE MEN NEED TO BE BRAVE ENOUGH TO TAKE A STAND.

69

My daughter embodies great self-respect and my hope is that
she will be treated accordingly. The examples we set in how we treat
our wives, our mothers, and our daughters are tremendously important.

I JUST WANT TO PROTECT HER FROM
ANYTHING THAT WOULD DAMPEN HER PASSION.
SHE IS SO FULL OF LIFE.

It takes a mature man to understand his emotions
and how to express them the right way.

JOSHUA CRIBBS

CLEVELAND BROWNS : WIDE RECEIVER

My little girl is very active, just like I was as a child. There is never a dull moment when I come home. She is definitely a "daddy's girl," and we have a lot of fun together. I just want to protect her from anything that would dampen her passion. She is so full of life.

I had a dream about my daughter before she was born, and I tell her about it all the time. I am as proud of her now as I was in my dreams.

Bringing home the money is not enough. My daughter won't remember that. I want her to remember our relationship and the fun stuff we do—playing hide-and-seek, doing homework, and having movie nights. Right now, we're making special memories.

It takes a mature man to understand his emotions and how to express them the right away. But we have to do that for our families and for future generations. I want more men to be accountable in their role as a father and as a man in society. Fathers are extremely important.

MATT HASSELBECK

SEATTLE SEAHAWKS : QUARTERBACK

Nurturing a relationship with your wife has nothing to do with letting a woman control you. True manhood is about sacrifice and being secure with who you are as a husband and father. I take my wife out on dates, show her affection, and make it a priority to spend time with her because it's important for me to show my daughters the love and respect they should expect from a man. Raising daughters is a huge responsibility and it's one that I don't take lightly.

My father worked hard to provide for us and always put his family first, which is how I learned to be a man. But I've seen guys who grew up without fathers make a decision to create a new legacy for their own family. The lesson here is that, despite what happened in the past, a man can find a great woman to marry and commit to loving and serving his family the way a real man should.

Raising daughters is a hugh responsibility and it's one that I don't take lightly.

TRUE MANHOOD IS ABOUT SACRIFICE AND
BEING SECURE WITH WHO YOU ARE
AS A HUSBAND AND FATHER.

MEN WHO DISRESPECT WOMEN MUST BE HELD ACCOUNTABLE.

My daughters are my precious angels.

RYAN PICKETT

GREEN BAY PACKERS : DEFENSIVE TACKLE

The most important role in my life is being a father. I am also lucky to have an amazing wife whom I respect and love. The women in my life are very special to me.

My daughters are my precious angels. I hope they grow up to be just like their mother.

Men who disrespect women must be held accountable. A real man takes responsibility to step in and say something before it is too late.

The women in my life are very special to me.

ROD WOODSON

Steelers, Ravens, Raiders : Former Player
NFL NETWORK : ANALYST

As men we need to talk about the way we feel, just like women do on a consistent basis. I think a lot of times we don't want to put our feelings out there, because if we say something to one of our buddies we're going to be seen as weak. I think true friends sit down and listen, and they try to help you in a positive manner and to influence you to do the right thing.

We are physically stronger than women, and I think at times we feel for some odd reason that we have to show that. That is not a real man. Men in general just need to understand that the best way to work a situation out is through talking and coming to a compromise.

In my third year in the NFL, my first daughter came along. It was probably the best thing for me because it made me see the world in a different light. Not only did I have to provide for me and my wife, but I had to provide for a little girl, my first daughter, my first child. For me, having a girl was the best thing because it made me have more compassion. I didn't have to be a rough and tough football player at home because little girls don't want or need that.

My kids don't see me as Hall of Famer Rod Woodson; I'm just dad. They say, "Hey Daddy" to me—that is a pure form of love. When kids put their hands up to you to hold them, it's like they're putting their hands up and surrendering to you, saying, "You're going to take care of me; I know I can trust you." I didn't take that for granted.

They're three beautiful girls, and I have big dreams for them to do the right thing and be successful in their lives. My role as a father is to show them how I treat their mother —with respect, dignity, and honor. Everything we do, we do as a partnership. Hopefully that can help them understand what they should be looking for in a husband.

For me, having a girl was the best thing because
it made me have more compassion.

MEN NEED TO UNDERSTAND THAT THE BEST WAY
TO WORK A SITUATION OUT IS THROUGH TALKING
AND COMING TO A COMPROMISE.

THE SMILES ON THEIR FACES ARE BETTER THAN

ANY GIFT I COULD EVER RECEIVE. I LOVE THEM DEEPLY.

RYAN CLARK

PITTSBURGH STEELERS : SAFETY

My daughters are true inspirations. Every day that I see them, I am motivated to be more and to do more so that I can secure a positive future for them. I love them deeply.

When I get home from work, both of my daughters greet me with outstretched arms as if I've been gone for months. I am truly blessed to have that experience each day. The smiles on their faces are better than any gift I could ever receive.

I hope that the thoughts of players in this book will allow young men to see that aggression has its time and place—on the field, not in relationships. I also hope it sends the message to young women that there are men out there who will love and respect them in the manner God intended.

I hope this book sends the message to young women that there are men who will love and respect them.

T.J. HOUSHMANZADEH

SEATTLE SEAHAWKS : WIDE RECEIVER

A man should walk away when his temper is getting the best of him. I would step in to save a woman from a bad situation, but also help the man, too. Domestic violence ruins the lives of everybody involved.

I am very outspoken, so friend or not, I encourage the men around me to treat women like they want to see men treat their mothers, daughters, and sisters. To me it's basic. It's about respecting yourself and having good intentions with other people.

I teach my daughters to be respectful to everybody and expect the same in return, especially from males. I love the hell out of them and want them to grow up with a good life and not be disrespected—verbally or physically—by anyone. Having girls definitely makes you take a look in the mirror to make sure you're on point. My daughters changed my life.

My daughters changed my life.

A MAN SHOULD WALK AWAY WHEN HIS TEMPER

IS GETTING THE BEST OF HIM.

Welcome

ENTERTAIN   ACCEPT

EMBRACE

A M U S E

SHARE

ENTRUST

FRIEND | CONFIDANT

The relationship between a father and daughter
should be a loving and open relationship.

— DAVID DIEHL

MY DAUGHTERS HAVE OPENED ME UP AND GIVEN ME

A BETTER PERSPECTIVE ON LIFE. THEY MAKE ME FEEL

LIKE THE MOST BLESSED MAN IN THE WORLD!

ADALIUS THOMAS

NEW ENGLAND PATRIOTS : LINEBACKER

When I am with my daughters, time seems to fly by. They are precious and grow up so fast. Even though I can spoil them at times, I try to balance that by also teaching them to have a strong mind and good work ethic. I want them to be genuinely kind to their peers, but I do not want them to be considered push-overs simply because they are girls.

As athletes, we have been ingrained by coaches, teammates, and fans to never let our guard down and to never show weakness. But having a little girl brings out the "teddy bear" in most players. My daughters have opened me up and given me a better perspective on life. They make me feel like the most blessed man in the world!

When I am with my daughters, time seems to fly by.

SHAUN SMITH

CINCINNATI BENGALS : DEFENSIVE TACKLE

Being a dad forced me to mature and prioritize the important aspects of life. I remember when my first child was born. I was going into training camp and the media reported that I might not make the team that year. My daughter gave me the motivation to focus and work harder because I knew that playing would allow my wife and me to provide her with the future we dreamed about. I realized then that my decisions would have an effect on my kids, so I vowed to give everything I have every day. But the best part of it all is knowing that even on my bad days, I can still count on the tender smiles on their faces, and it makes me proud to be a father.

More men should take pride in being a reliable father and a good man in general. Amongst each other, our conversations should be about taking care of our family, spoiling the women in our lives, and exercising control when we are frustrated or stressed instead of bragging about sexual escapades. If we all keep our daughters in mind, we'll be more conscious of the company we keep and know why it's important, not to only model appropriate behavior consistently, but also to address unacceptable behavior.

I think this book is necessary to get other men involved in taking a stand against domestic violence. For those who may not have a suitable father figure in the home, hopefully our voice will inspire them to identify a good man to emulate. Likewise, I hope more good men reach out to the younger generation and help build the men who we'd consider to be acceptable for our daughters.

My daughter is independent,

and I love that about her.

JEFF SATURDAY

INDIANAPOLIS COLTS : CENTER

My daughter is independent, and I love that about her. She is a very dynamic girl and the star of my life. She loves when I take her somewhere special, like dinner dates with just the two of us. She just wants to spend time with me, and I believe that is the best way to show her how a man is supposed to treat her—the way I treat her momma. I pray that she finds happiness and joy in her life.

One thing I have learned as I have grown up in this game is that aggressiveness and the mentality to intimidate another human being is really just a facade; it's just for show. I want men to understand that what we put on the field is a game, and it's not how we live our lives off the field. I don't need to use intimidation as a measure of respect in my life.

I PRAY THAT SHE FINDS HAPPINESS
AND JOY IN HER LIFE.

DARREN SHARPER

NEW ORLEANS SAINTS : SAFETY

I have thoroughly enjoyed watching my daughter grow up. She is a bright spot in my life, and thinking about her helps me stay focused. As my first born, she is definitely special, and I am thankful for the positive influence she has had on me. Sacrificing for her instilled selflessness in me that I know I wouldn't have gotten any other way. Playing football can be glamorous at times, but being a father keeps me humble. I love her unconditionally, and I make it a point keep the lines of communication open between us so that she knows she can talk to me about anything.

My daughter makes my mindful of how women are treated, undervalued, and exploited, which is why I felt compelled to take advantage of this opportunity to speak up about domestic violence. Money cannot buy the women we love everyday security, which men take for granted. So, it's going to take strong, accountable men to educate young boys and influence other men to deal with women respectfully, honorably, and fairly at all times. Taking care of the women in our family is vitally important, but our daughters cannot stay home forever. This is why, as men, we must take care of the world we live in as well.

Money cannot buy the women we love everyday security, which men take for granted.

PLAYING FOOTBALL CAN BE GLAMOROUS AT TIMES,
BUT BEING A FATHER KEEPS ME HUMBLE.

I KEEP HER IN MIND IN EVERYTHING I DO.

DAVID THORNTON

TENNESSEE TITANS : LINEBACKER

My daughter accelerated my development as a man. When she was born, she became my priority. I keep her in mind in everything I do. It's been a true pleasure watching her grow into a delightful, intelligent young lady who loves God and her dad.

I am supporting this cause because I want to encourage other fathers, whether single or married, to stay involved in the lives of their children. The time I spend with my daughter is important, because I show her that she is valuable and should be treated accordingly. I take pride in being the best father I can be to my daughter, but I also want to be an example for young men. Fathers have a key role in helping kids develop into good people.

Manhood is not about money or sexual conquests although television and music leads you to believe so. The messages can be confusing for a lot of young guys, but real men need to stand up and set the standard. Being a man is about integrity, responsibility, being a good father, respecting women, and faithfully serving God.

The time I spend with my daughter is important, because I show her that she is valuable and should be treated accordingly.

DAVID DIEHL

NEW YORK GIANTS : OFFENSIVE LINEMAN

Even though I'm a guy who is 6'6" and 300 pounds, I just crumble when I see my daughter's face or when she gives me a hug. My favorite memory is when she came to her first game (Giants vs. Raiders) and she was able to see me play. She was in a little cheerleader outfit and my brother, who was in town for the game, lifted her on his shoulders so she could see me. When she waved and smiled at me, it was the best thing.

As a parent and a father, I want my daughter to have all the opportunities in the world to be successful. I want to lead by example and show her how to be a good person in the community by always being nice and respectful. I want her to learn that she needs to dedicate herself to whatever she decides to do and commit herself to working as hard as she can in order to accomplish her goals.

The birth of my daughter gave me purpose and a vision for what life is really all about. When I became a parent, I realized that it wasn't about me anymore. She helps me put things into a better perspective. The relationship between a father and daughter should be a loving and open relationship. I want her to be happy with whatever she chooses to do with her life, and I want to give her the best opportunities. My job is to be there for her, to help guide her in the right direction, and to give her the confidence to know that she can do anything.

I WANT HER TO BE HAPPY
WITH WHATEVER SHE CHOOSES TO DO WITH
HER LIFE, AND I WANT TO GIVE HER THE BEST OPPORTUNITIES.

The relationship between a father and daughter
should be a loving and open relationship.

I CHOOSE TO BE AN EXAMPLE.

KELLEN CLEMENS

NEW YORK JETS : QUARTERBACK

Words can only go so far. It's your actions that really sink in with young people. You can talk until you are blue in the face, but if you don't have the actions to back it up, it's going to go completely unheard. I choose to be an example, not only for my son, but for my son's friends because not everyone is raised in an ideal environment. Challenging the norm, doing the right thing, and being an example of what it really means to be a man are the first steps in stopping abuse against women.

The greatest joy I get each day is when I come home from work and see my daughter's face light up as I come through the door. She just comes running with her hands held out for a great big hug. It's something I really look forward to every day.

The greatest joy I get each day is when I come home from work and see my daughter's face light up as I come through the door.

JAMES THRASH

REDSKINS, EAGLES : FORMER PLAYER

I really like to sit down with all my girls at the end of each day. I want to make sure that I'm listening to them. I want to hear everything big, small, good, or bad—every situation they go through is important to me. My goal is develop the communication, so that as they get older, we can still have an open relationship. If they have any problem or issue, they will know that they can come and talk to Daddy.

For the sake of my daughters, I hope this project will inspire men to change their behavior. As athletes, we can set a huge example of what other men can model their lives after, because many people think of us as the ideal representation of manhood. To show that we can be involved in an aggressive sport but still treat the special women in our lives with love and tenderness is valuable. There are always going to be people looking at us. Coach Gibbs would always say, "The biggest thing you can leave in life is the impact you left on others." I think for me, the impact that I want to leave is what a man should look like, a good man. That's the type of legacy I want to leave, not only for my family, but for society as well.

I HOPE THIS PROJECT WILL INSPIRE MEN TO CHANGE THEIR BEHAVIOR.

My goal is to develop the communication,
so that as they get older,
we can still have an open relationship.

I tell our daughters all the time to stand up
for what they believe in.

AS MEN, WE MUST SET AN EXAMPLE AMONG OURSELVES.
SILENCE SIGNIFIES ACCEPTANCE, BUT SPEAKING OUT SHOWS COURAGE.

COACH RON TURNER

INDIANAPOLIS COLTS : WIDE RECEIVERS COACH

Women can do any job that a man can do, and they should be treated with the same respect. My daughters are the main reason I wanted to be part of this special project. I know how important it is for all of society to give them an equal chance. I want everyone to treat my daughters right in working relationships and personal relationships as well. I believe that is the hope of every loving father, and we all must deal with the issue in order for that to happen.

My wife and I tell our daughters all the time to stand up for what they believe in. No woman should tolerate anything but being treated with the utmost respect.

As men, we must set an example amongst ourselves. The way we talk about women in the work place, or wherever it may be, we need to have the courage to show that it's okay to be sensitive and it's okay to have compassion. You don't have to come across as a macho man who has to prove that he's tough by devaluing a woman. A confident man, without hidden insecurities, should be able to challenge and influence his counterparts who have issues with respecting women. Silence signifies acceptance, but speaking out shows courage.

JOEY PORTER

ARIZONA CARDINALS : LINEBACKER

I want my daughters to be happy and to always take pride in being a part of this family! I want them to feel loved every single day, and I want them to know they can come to my wife and me at anytime, for any reason. They deserve to be respected. Anything that's harmful to them, emotionally or physically, is completely unacceptable.

I know that my kids watch everything I do and they try to emulate me, so I always make decisions that I would want them to make.

As professional athletes, we have a platform that lets us reach, and perhaps inspire, a large audience. We must never condone the degradation of women. This disrespect often stems from a man's own insecurities. Men who put their hands on a woman are cowards. Unfortunately, a lot of men learn at a young age that if you like a female you should put her down. But if we teach men how to deal with their own feelings, hopefully we can stop this cycle.

I WANT THEM TO FEEL LOVED EVERY SINGLE DAY, AND I WANT THEM TO KNOW THEY CAN COME TO MY WIFE AND ME AT ANYTIME.

They deserve to be respected.

The relationship between a father and
a daughter needs to be celebrated.

SCOTTIE GRAHAM

Vikings, Jets, Bengals : Former Player

NFL PLAYERS ASSOCIATION : REGIONAL DIRECTOR

The relationship between a father and a daughter needs to be celebrated because a daughter's first love is the love of her father.

My daughter is 13 and funny as all get out. I spend as much time with her as I can even if that means leaving work early. I pick her up from ballet just because. I want people to know that she has an involved father, and I also want her to understand that she is very important to me.

I WANT PEOPLE TO KNOW THAT SHE HAS AN
        INVOLVED FATHER, AND I ALSO WANT HER TO
    UNDERSTAND THAT SHE IS VERY IMPORTANT TO ME.

ORLANDO PACE

CHICAGO BEARS : OFFENSIVE TACKLE

My daughter is visibly excited every time she sees me and that makes me feel good, no matter what kind of day I had. She is my princess, and I look forward to her hugs and kisses every morning when she wakes up and every night before she goes to bed. When I come home from work hurt, she'll be the first to say, "Daddy, are you okay?" She is so compassionate and loving.

We love to laugh together, and I appreciate every moment we share. They are all special.

I tell my daughter to dream big, and I want her to grow up in a world where she has the opportunity to do so. I consider myself to be her role model, but as a football player, I know I am a role model for other young people as well.

Other players can also influence the next generation by being positive and respectful towards all women at all times.

We love to laugh together,
and I appreciate every moment we share.

I TELL MY DAUGHTER TO DREAM BIG, AND I WANT HER TO GROW UP
IN A WORLD WHERE SHE HAS THE OPPORTUNITY TO DO SO.

I thank God for my daughters, because they are incredibly special

and loyal and love me unconditionally.

BERTRAND BERRY

ARIZONA CARDINALS : DEFENSIVE END

Growing up, I always envisioned that I would have sons. I think I was mentally prepared for having a boy because, like most men, I dreamt of tossing the ball around in the yard and roughhousing with a little version of myself. Although I was blessed to eventually have a son, having a daughter first was a life-changing experience. I believe that I am a better father today because my first-born daughter taught me how to be more sensitive and let my guard down and to get in touch with a side of myself that I had yet to explore. She made it okay for me to be a strong man who can also be expressive and vulnerable at times.

I thank God for my daughters, because they are incredibly special and loyal and love me unconditionally. I savor each and every memory we create with our private time away from the rest of the family, and I know how important is it to just listen to what is on their minds. Even their spirituality has encouraged me to get closer to God. To hear my daughters pray for me and read the Bible moves me beyond measure, and I know that God had good reason to bless with me with both of them. It is clear that I need them just as much as they need me.

As a devoted father who wants a better world for his daughters, I think it's important for my voice to be heard on the issue of domestic violence. All men are to blame for not speaking out about this issue more, especially for those of us who have daughters. We need to speak up and out, hold each other accountable, and take a long, hard look in the mirror to make sure that we are blameless. Tasteless jokes, embellished stories about encounters with women, and being silent when we know that a man is mistreating a woman are contributing factors and must stop for positive change. Aggression and dominance have no place in a relationship with a woman. That behavior should be reserved for sports and competition, as it is the only appropriate place.

SCOTT FUJITA

CLEVELAND BROWNS : LINEBACKER

I think of myself as a pretty hands-on father. My wife describes me as "another mother." With twins, you need all hands on deck from day one, and I think my wife and I make a pretty good team. Some guys might find that emasculating, but I'm quite proud of it.

One of the great things about being a father is that when you wake up in the morning, you know that each day has the potential to create a new favorite memory. There's clearly a special connection between twins, and it's rewarding to see how thoughtful and caring they are toward each other.

More than anything else, I just want them to be happy. I want them to feel loved every single day, and I want them to know they can come to me or my wife at anytime, for any reason. I want them to be fearless. I want them to have the confidence to attempt anything, even if it seems impossible. I want them to recognize how bright their futures are. I want them to feel empowered to make their own decisions—not for anyone else, but for themselves. I want them to believe that they can do anything.

MORE THAN ANYTHING ELSE, I JUST WANT THEM TO BE HAPPY.

When you wake up in the morning, you know that
each day has the potential to create a new favorite memory.

I understand how important it is for me
to listen to her and be there for her.

THE IDEA THAT "MEN ARE JUST BEING MEN" SO BAD BEHAVIOR
SHOULD BE ACCEPTED NEEDS TO BE REVERSED.

TYRONE KNOTT

SAN FRANCICO 49ERS : DIRECTOR OF PLAYER DEVELOPMENT

What interested me about this project is the very special relationship that is shared between a father and a daughter. Every time my daughter asks, "Daddy, when are you coming home from work?" I understand how important it is for me to listen to her and be there for her. It's that feeling that led me to be a part of this book. This is a great opportunity.

The idea that "men are just being men" so bad behavior should be accepted needs to be reversed. Even if you grew up seeing women being treated as objects or hearing men talk down to women, it's time to learn the right way to behave. When I work with players, I always emphasize the importance of respecting and honoring their commitment to a woman, just as they do to the game of football.

I have a relationship with the Lord, which sets the groundwork in order for me to be the man that I want to be for my daughter, my wife, and my sons. Each day, I pray that I am able to live up to the standard He has set for my life so that I can be an example for the people around me.

BELIEVE

PRAISE

APPLAUD

Excite

STRENGTHEN

BOOST

ENCOURAGE

CHAMPION | FAN

No parent is perfect, and being a good father takes work.

— BRENDON AYANBADEJO

MY HOPE IS THAT SHE CAN CONTINUE TO BE THAT FREE SPIRIT FOREVER.

To be able to see your daughter in a purely authentic,
non-staged moment, where she is absolutely thrilled to be exactly
where she wants to be doing exactly what she wants, is beautiful.

DEMAURICE SMITH

NFL PLAYERS ASSOCIATION : EXECUTIVE DIRECTOR

My daughter is special, caring, interesting, funny, unique, brilliant, and tough—she's all of those things and more.

She's fun, and I get to coach her in basketball, as I have for the last four years. So we not only have a great father-daughter relationship, but we also have a really cool player-coach relationship. It's special to have that with your daughter. She probably takes the worst of it being the coach's daughter, but she always rises to the challenge. That's what makes her a really special person to love, live with, and coach.

There's a picture on my desk of her at the White House Easter Egg Roll, when she had gone off by herself. It was a beautiful day, and she's there with her arms out looking up to the sky, twirling around. To be able to see your daughter in a purely authentic, non-staged moment, where she is absolutely thrilled to be exactly where she wants to be doing exactly what she wants, is beautiful. My hope is that she can continue to be that free spirit forever.

I want my daughter to be as happy when she grows up as we were the day that she was born.

COACH TONY DUNGY

Steelers, Raiders : Former Player | Buccaneers, Colts : Former Coach

NBC SPORTS : ANALYST

My job as a father is to be a role model and help my daughters grow into young women. Obviously moms do a lot in that regard, but I think dads do that as well—by being there and being protective and by demonstrating what you hope they look for in men as they grow and become mature women.

My dad did a great job with my sisters and encouraged them to think outside the box and do things they would enjoy. I have one sister who is a nurse and one sister who is a doctor, and my dad encouraged them to think about what they wanted to do in the future. That is what I hope I do for my daughters, so that they are not inhibited by any preconceived ideas of what they can do as women. I would also like them to experience the type of relationship that my wife and I have—for them to know that they can find husbands who would complement them and help them grow. That would be ideal.

We need to show young men today what it is like to be a real man, to expose your feelings, to be considerate of other people, and all those other characteristics that may not be highlighted on the football field. So many of our players and other young men didn't see that husband-wife relationship from their parents and never really understood what that was like. I think we need to highlight the importance of the father-daughter relationship and how much our daughters gain by having their dads take an active role in their lives. I think the more we have our guys speaking about it, the more we are going to raise that level of awareness.

I THINK WE NEED TO HIGHLIGHT THE IMPORTANCE
OF THE FATHER-DAUGHTER RELATIONSHIP AND HOW
MUCH DAUGHTERS GAIN BY HAVING THEIR DADS TAKE
AN ACTIVE ROLE IN THEIR LIVES.

My dad did a great job with my sisters and
encouraged them to think outside the box.
That is what I hope I do for my daughters.

NO PARENT IS PERFECT, AND BEING A GOOD FATHER TAKES WORK.
MEN CAN'T TAKE BREAKS, AS IT TAKES
DAY-TO-DAY PRACTICE TO BE THE BEST.

BRENDON AYANBADEJO

BALTIMORE RAVENS : LINEBACKER

Society tends to highlight the role of a mother when it comes to parenting. But when my daughter was born, I was determined to have equal involvement in her life. It's the little things that I experience in raising her that are so special, those unforgettable moments that I wouldn't trade for the world. She continues to change me and help me grow into a better man. Being her father has made me more affectionate, loving, patient, and sensitive. It also made me more responsible because caring for her and making sure her needs are met makes me understand the important things in life. I cherish her childhood and want to be there for her at all times.

Becoming a great father can be a learning process, and I credit Coach Harbaugh and my teammate Ray Lewis for influencing me when they probably didn't even know it. Even before my daughter was born, they both talked about the importance of family and making those responsibilities a priority. They consistently backed their words up with actions, and I respect them both so much for that. I hope that my actions as a father will leave the same impression on those who are around me.

No parent is perfect, and being a good father takes work. Men can't take breaks, as it takes day-to-day practice to be the best. The same holds true for being the best man you can be. You can't treat your mother or sister one way and treat your girlfriend or wife a different way. Every woman is worthy of respect, and if more men would embrace that idea and actually live it, the better chance we have at changing the world and ending violence against women.

MATT LIGHT

NEW ENGLAND PATRIOTS : OFFENSIVE TACKLE

Your first child always holds a special place in your heart. But when you have a girl first, it really makes you more aware of your responsibility as a man and as a father—especially when you are a 6'4", 300-pound football player. With a long NFL season, it's easy to get caught up in the hustle and bustle of everyday life without taking time to reflect on and appreciate the important things. I appreciate my children because they are a daily reminder of how lucky I am. My daughter and I have a very trusting relationship, and I will never take that for granted. No matter what the situation is, I love her and support her unconditionally.

I realize that my daughter may be exposed to things in life that are out of my control. But I strive to surround her and my other children with other positive men. In order to learn what it means for a strong man to respect and treat a woman the right way, they need to see other men besides their father doing the right thing. My hope is that all men will embrace that responsibility and do a better job at modeling for the sake of my daughters and the daughters of others.

This project is important to me, not only because it showcases the men of the NFL who aren't recognized enough for being great fathers, but also because it sends a message to the kids out there who look up to us and need to see that our lives are about more than what they see on Sunday. As an athlete, I feel blessed to be in this position where I can impact what it means to be a father and a man.

I APPRECIATE MY CHILDREN BECAUSE THEY ARE A DAILY
REMINDER OF HOW LUCKY I AM.

My daughter and I have a very trusting
relationship, and I will never take that for granted.

I AM SO MUCH MORE THAN A FOOTBALL PLAYER.
I AM A DAD WHO LOVES EVERY PART OF BEING A FATHER

Modeling for young people is the key,

but modeling for our peers is important as well.

TONY STEWART

OAKLAND RAIDERS : TIGHT END

People have a natural interest in my relationship with my sons because I am a football player. So it is an honor and privilege for this opportunity to focus on the extraordinary bond I have with my daughter. Playing in the NFL has allowed me to do many things with young people in the community, but talking about my daughter is a great angle for them to really understand the values I represent in my family life. I am so much more than a football player. I am a dad who loves every part of being a father. My daughter warms my heart and brings a smile to my face every time I see her.

To be sure that I didn't mishandle my responsibility as her father, I opened up the Bible and relied on its principles to guide me. My daughter is so delicate, sweet, and innocent. I definitely want to protect her from harm, but I know that I can't shelter her forever. This is why I believe that my role as a man, modeling appropriate behavior in the community, is an important part of affecting the world in which she lives. More accountable, responsible men should be at the forefront of defining manhood for society rather than reality TV, which depicts women as objects and subordinate to men.

Modeling for young people is the key, but modeling for our peers is important as well. There comes a point when certain "jokes" and embellished stories about relationships with women (which are often times untrue) are unacceptable. As men, we need to grow out of that and be brave enough to tell other men to just stop.

CASEY RABACH

I hope that this book sends a message that violence against women is not okay. It's just wrong and more men need to speak out about it. Staying quiet is like accepting the fact that it happens. I'm really glad to be a part of this project because I feel very strongly about this issue.

Just because women may not be as big or strong as some males, that doesn't make them inferior to men. There are a lot of great qualities about women. We need to look at those, embrace them and cherish them.

I definitely want the men in my daughter's life to be respectful of who she is as an individual and to value her capabilities. As she grows up, I want someone who cares for her well-being and knows that she is important.

There are a lot of great qualities about women.
We need to look at those,
embrace them, and cherish them.

I DEFINITELY WANT THE MEN IN MY DAUGHTER'S LIFE
TO BE RESPECTFUL OF WHO SHE IS AS AN INDIVIDUAL
AND TO VALUE HER CAPABILITIES.

IT'S SAD THAT WE LOSE SIGHT OF HOW IMPORTANT
AND STRONG WOMEN ARE IN SOCIETY.

DeANGELO HALL

WASHINGTON REDSKINS : CORNERBACK

There is a special bond between a father and his daughter. I hold myself to a high standard with my daughter so that one day she will not settle for anything less than what her dad was! And if I succeed at my job, I think I'll be able to sleep at night.

All men come from a woman. It takes two, but women carry a child for nine months and then give birth to the child. I think it's sad that we lose sight of how important and strong women in society are.

I hold myself to a high standard with my daughter so that one day she will not settle for anything less.

DEON GRANT

SEATTLE SEAHAWKS : SAFETY

Some men choose not to confront domestic violence because they think they're good guys, so it's not their problem. But in the long run, we aren't going to be around forever to protect our little girls. We should all consider it our problem because we have the power to affect the world they live in now and possibly impact the future.

Resorting to violence is a sign of weakness, especially when the other person cannot physically defend herself. Exhibiting self-control is what it means to be strong.

I am a God-fearing man who respects the importance and vitality of women. Women give life; they make the world turn. I have respect for all of them; not just my family members, but all women.

I am a hands-on father and try to spend as much time with my daughter as I can. She is special and inspires me to surpass being a good father—I want to be great!

I am a hands-on father and try to spend as much time with my daughter as I can.

WE HAVE THE POWER TO AFFECT
THE WORLD IN WHICH THEY LIVE NOW.

131

WE HAVE TO TAKE MORE RESPONSIBILITY
FOR WHAT WE DO AND SAY AND MAKE MORE
OF AN EFFORT TO SPEND QUALITY TIME WITH OUR KIDS.

TAKEO SPIKES

SAN FRANCISO 49ERS : LINEBACKER

My daughter adds purpose and direction to my life. Even when we're not together, I am thinking about her and making plans for the future. My love for her is infinite, and the impact she's had on my personal growth as a man is phenomenal. My decisions are definitely more calculated with her in mind. I often compare parenting to gardening. You have to prepare the plot, nurture the plant, keep out the weeds, and be ready for unpredictable weather. Similarly, I strive to be in tune with the ever-changing needs of my daughter so that I can give her what she needs to flourish.

I want the boys and men in her future to understand that she is valuable. More men need to be active in the lives of younger men because they will eventually be interacting with somebody's daughter. The kind of tough love my parents showed me should be extended so that inappropriate behavior toward women stops. We cannot turn a blind eye to violence when we know that there's a better way to handle difficult situations. Kids will naturally be kids, but learning to be a responsible adult can only come from other responsible adults. I am honored to be among other concerned fathers in this book who are taking on that responsibility.

Knowledge is meant to be passed on so that others can benefit from you the things you have learned. I take this approach with my daughter each time we are together. It's nice to have fun and play games; we do that a lot. But steering her growth and ensuring that she is prepared to be successful in life is very important to me as well. During the off-season, we are inseparable, and I love that we enjoy spending time together. Whether we're swimming and hosting sleepovers with her friends or she's on business trips with me, there is a lesson to be learned in every aspect of what we do. My favorite thing about being her father is seeing her implement the things that I've taught her.

JAY FEELY

NEW YORK JETS : KICKER

As a father, my job is to protect my daughters, emulate how a man should treat them, and encourage them to utilize all the gifts God gave them to achieve their dreams. My daughters' relationships with men will be defined by the role I play in their lives.

My daughters are leaders, each with outgoing, vibrant personalities. They are my princesses. I try to encourage my teammates to respect the women they date and to be aware that each woman is someone else's princess, someone else's daughter, and they have the same desires for their daughter that I have for mine.

This past summer my wife and I took our kids kayaking. We got out to explore an island and, to the delight of my girls, we found a bounty of wild, ripe blueberries. The girls ate to their hearts' content and had the unencumbered joy that I hope to see in their lives forever. That is what a father wants for his daughter: unencumbered joy and dreams fulfilled for a lifetime.

My daughters are leaders, each with outgoing, vibrant personalities. They are my princesses.

THAT IS WHAT A FATHER WANTS FOR HIS DAUGHTER:
UNENCUMBERED JOY AND DREAMS FULFILLED FOR A LIFETIME.

They don't just see me as a football player;
they see me as a dad. That brings me great joy.

MARK BRUENER

STEELERS, TEXANS : FORMER PLAYER

A great thing about my relationship with my daughters is that they don't just see me as a football player; they see me as a dad. They don't care if Daddy wins or loses, and they don't care what's going on in my work life. All they care about is if Daddy is home.

Although football is a very rough and tough sport, when I go home I try to leave as much as I can at the stadium. When I get home, I have to show compassion and kindness and be gentle with my daughters.

By participating in this book, I want to show that even though I am a rough-and-tough football player and I've played this game for 14 years, I still am a human being, and I have a family that I care for and want to nurture. It's not okay for a husband to speak unkindly to his wife or even raise his voice. How I choose to speak to my wife is my way of modeling what I want my girls to look for when they are older.

WHEN I GET HOME, I HAVE TO SHOW COMPASSION AND KINDNESS AND BE GENTLE WITH MY DAUGHTERS.

MIKE FURREY

CLEVELAND BROWNS : WIDE RECEIVER

Work is work, but when you go home, real life begins. The relationship with your kids will last a lifetime. Football may only last a few years. I would rather my daughter remember me not for being a great football player but for being a great father.

When we were shooting photos for this project, it was just me and her in a little circle, and we didn't care about the camera. We were having fun with each other; laughing, giggling, me tickling her and her tickling me—just enjoying each other.

My daughter sets the example for her brothers. We tell her that she is in a position to teach them, because they look up to her and are always watching. I want my daughter to grow up in a world where she can continue to be a leader.

Work is work. But when you go home, real life begins.
The relationship with your kids will last a lifetime.

I WANT MY DAUGHTER TO GROW UP IN A WORLD
WHERE SHE CAN CONTINUE TO BE A LEADER.

WE HAVE TO TAKE MORE RESPONSIBILITY
FOR WHAT WE DO AND SAY AND MAKE MORE
OF AN EFFORT TO SPEND QUALITY TIME WITH OUR KIDS.

NA'IL DIGGS

CAROLINA PANTHERS : OUTSIDE LINEBACKER

There's nothing like having a daughter, which is why this topic hit home for me. It is important for me to be a great father to my daughter, to be active in her life, to guide her through the ups and downs. Athletes are not just figures on TV; we're positive people with families who take our responsibilities seriously.

When men abandon families or demonstrate violence against women, young men naturally pick up negative behavior. It comes down to fathers today; we have to take more responsibility for what we do and say, and make more of an effort to spend quality time with our kids. Chasing women and talking about this girl and that girl in the locker room are not the qualities of a real man. Being a true leader and a real man means not making excuses for destructive behavior, rather it's more about becoming a part of the change that will have a positive effect on our children.

It is important for me to be a great father. There's nothing like having a daughter.

SAMARI ROLLE

BALTIMORE RAVENS : CORNERBACK

The birth of my daughters is my favorite memory. I remember thinking that I want them to admire me as a positive role model and an example of a father who is involved in their lives. I want them to appreciate this book and know that it is an expression of my love for them.

My daughters are smart and vibrant. They will accomplish whatever they set out to do as independent women.

I WANT THEM TO ADMIRE ME AS A POSITIVE ROLE MODEL

AND AN EXAMPLE OF A FATHER

WHO IS INVOLVED IN THEIR LIVES.

I have two daughters and they are both smart and vibrant.
They will accomplish whatever they
set out to do as independent women.

My hope is that she'll build relationships
with individuals who understand themselves
and the challenges of partnerships.

MIKE HAYNES

Patriots, Raiders : Former Player

FORMER NFL VICE PRESIDENT OF PLAYER DEVELOPMENT

In conversations that I've had with some men, they think the woman did something to deserve the abuse. So there's a lot of education that needs to take place. It may not be an easy conversation to have, but we have to communicate the idea that there is no right time to hit or abuse a woman. I encourage men to engage each other in open and honest dialogue about violence against women, so that all men can play a part in making sure that these problems don't continue.

I want my daughter to be safe, be healthy, and thrive in an environment where she can be successful. My hope is that she'll build relationships with individuals who understand themselves and the challenges of partnerships while being courageous enough to deal with those challenges appropriately.

I WANT MY DAUGHTER TO BE SAFE, BE HEALTHY

AND THRIVE IN AN ENVIRONMENT

WHERE SHE CAN BE SUCCESSFUL.

MATT WARE

ARIZONA CARDINALS : DEFENSIVE BACK

Coming home to my daughter gives me peace and helps me forget about any stress or issues from the day. Seeing her smile or hearing her giggle renews my energy, and I really enjoying being a father. I've grown immensely since her birth, and I just pray that God continues to give me wisdom so that I am able to give her all that she needs—materially, as well as emotionally.

I love my daughter for how she's helped me mature as a man. Being patient, loving, nurturing, sensitive, and even showing vulnerability when appropriate are things I've learned as a father. It's refreshing to express myself in this way knowing that I am free to do so, because my daughter loves me completely without judging.

Playing football or feeding into what society expects of a man implies that aggressiveness and dominance are necessary. However, this falsehood calls for more men to be leaders, not followers. Women have led the fight against domestic violence alone for way too long. I am honored to join my colleagues in making a statement. We want our mothers, wives, sisters, and daughters to be safe and receive the same respect that we expect for ourselves.

Seeing her smile or hearing her giggle renews my energy, and I really enjoying being a father.

WOMEN HAVE LED THE FIGHT AGAINST DOMESTIC VIOLENCE

ALONE FOR WAY TOO LONG. I AM HONORED

TO JOIN MY COLLEAGUES IN MAKING A STATEMENT.

PHOTO CREDITS

James Brown: Anita Bartlett | **Mark Bruener**: Christine Meeker Photography | **Andra Davis**: St. Peppers Photography

Brian Dawkins: Nancy Cohn Photography | **Na'il Diggs**: Carrie Reiser Photography | **Heath Evans**: Andrea Graeve

Mike Furrey: Elizabeth Ferraro | **La'Roi Glover**: Laura Siebert | **Deangelo Hall**: Amy Maffei, SugarSnapps Photography

Matt Hasslebeck: Nigel Parry, Canon | **Torry Holt**: Laura Siebert | **Donovan McNabb**: Jody Robinson | **Orlando Pace**: Laura Siebert

Joey Porter: Scott Hislop Photography | **Samari Rolle**: J Lash | **Brian Waters**: Haynesworth Photography

DeMarcus Ware: Amy Headington, Grace Photography | **Ryan Pickett**: The Picture People, 211 Bay Park Square Green Bay, WI 54304

Tony Stewart: Pam Biasotti Photography | **Jake Delhomme**: Brent LeBlanc at Allen Breaux Studio | **Jerome Bettis**: Paul Wharton

Scottie Graham: Stephanie Millner Photography | **Kevin Mawae**: Karma Hill, Good Karma Photography | **DeMaurice Smith**: Kevin Koski

Matt Ware: Our365 Portraits | **Deshea Townsend**: The Picture People | **Walt Harris**: A. Withers Photo Gallery

NOTE: The images in this book were provided by the men of the NFL, and every attempt was made to correctly identify the photographers. In the event that an appropriate credit was omitted, please accept our apologies—and our thanks for supporting this important project.

Copyright © 2010 by NFL Players Association

No part of this publication may be reproduced, stored in a retrieval system, or transmitted in any form by any means, electronic, mechanical, photocopying, or otherwise, without the prior written permission of the publisher, Triumph Books, 542 South Dearborn Street, Suite 750, Chicago, Illinois 60605.

Triumph Books and colophon are registered trademarks of Random House, Inc.

This book is available in quantity at special discounts for your group or organization. For further information, contact:

TRIUMPH BOOKS

542 South Dearborn Street

Suite 750

Chicago, Illinois 60605

(312) 939-3330

Fax (312) 663-3557

www.triumphbooks.com

Printed in Canada

ISBN: 978-1-60078-499-6

Cover design and additional page design/production by Paul Petrowsky
Jacket photos: **Torry Holt**: Laura Siebert, **Jerome Bettis**: Paul Wharton, **Matt Hasslebeck**: Nigel Parry, Canon, **James Brown**: Anita Bartlett